Other Books by Sandra Sidman Larson

Chapbooks

Whistling Girls and Cackling Hens 2003 (Sandra Jane Larson)
Over the Threshold of Roots 2007 (Sandra Jane Larson)
Weekend Weather: Calendar Poems 2011
Ode to Beautiful 2016

Books

This Distance in My Hands 2017
With No Intention of Arrival 2021

And Now
What Shall We Do?

A Memoir in Poetry by Sandra Sidman Larson

CUP AND SPIRAL BOOKS
MINNEAPOLIS  MINNESOTA

In memory of Blanche Rice

CONTENTS

Awakening

Kindness sits in the branches of despair.
Is there anything
that will allow grief to bear
its burden? A small hand sticks up
from under rubble built
by bombs.
The old woman stirs her empty
pot of sorrow.
A few birds
in a nearby bush are singing.
Can you hear them?

After Naomi Shihab Nye

Sandra ("Sandy"), 20 months old,
Misquamicut, Rhode Island, August 1938

On a Rhode Island Beach

August 1938

A toddler sits near the crest
of the past, unconcerned
by the ocean's vast expanse.
She is busy with a red and yellow toy crane,
filling a small shovel with sand.
Her father, resting on his haunches,
guides her hand to dump it into the crane's
bucket and shows her how to crank
the handle to put the bucket into position
to drop its load of sand onto the unfinished
walls of a sandcastle—a sandcastle
she will continue to rebuild
for the rest of her life.

What Remains

Misquamicut, Rhode Island

1954

Wild rose bushes growing again, briars
and bayberries underfoot. This is
the first time either Mother or I
have returned here. She points to
scattered boulders.

> *Those are from basements*
> *or retaining walls. I think our house   was   here.*
> *I don't know. It was so long ago . . .*

The stones now purposed as sentinels
survey an amusement park, its Tilt-A-Whirl
and hot dog stand posted on a sandy strip
once heavily plotted with turn-of-the-century
cottages. No dunes left to climb,
hydrangeas line the rebuilt boardwalk.

> *Mother, what can you tell me?*
> *Do you remember?*

A toddler then, I can recall only faded tidbits
of emotions, sights, and smells—like the salt air,
the sand between my toes—and yet I am tied
to this place, like an umbilical cord,
something discarded unknown, but vital.

1938

A car rumbles into the drive, quiets,
curtains stir in the August breeze.
Back from work her daddy enters
the small child's room, lifts her
into the light of late afternoon,
places her back into the buttery sun.

> After supper, on the front porch, rocking
> into evening, the family relaxes.
> The sun falls away, waves darken,
> and gulls pick at the scene, swooping
> up and down the beach.

Then everyone moving, Grandmother Nana packing up
the family belongings, folding items, stowing
what's to stay, while Grandfather Awah stashes
the fishing nets against the basement wall.

> All this activity, all this preparation done
> without realizing disaster is coming,
> a devastating hurricane just weeks away,
> arriving unannounced after their family
> and many neighbors are gone.

Miles away, after the storm hits, the family sees
pictures in the newspaper of a codfish-colored sky
turned barrel heavy, and on the radio hears how
the rain set in, and the wind raged,
blowing out windows, doors, the cottages

    cracking at their joints, collapsing
    under the weight of water, disappearing
    out to sea, the New England coast decimated,
    their Misquamicut swept completely away,

a place where people had come to rub shoulders
with the sea. This spit of sand was built up with homes
to harbor those privileged enough to rest
in nature's good graces. Afterwards,

    the lucky survivors tell stories—
    how they drove off in time, or
    (a few of them) rode away
    miraculously on the detached
    upper floors of their houses.

Finally, the survivors tell devastating stories
of the not so lucky, like a maid, dressed
in her Sunday best who stood on the porch waving
to her family who did not squeeze her

    into the family Ford as they left, promising
    to come back for her.
    And as the family drove away,
    they saw her suddenly swept off
    the porch by a massive wave—gone—

only her blue hat with its upright
green feather left on the surface
as it rode swirling away,
swirling away

    into the suffering nights of the bereaved,
    mixing the depth of loss with the looming
    images of a world war soon to break out,
    swirling away into the onslaught of history.

Few structures remain post-hurricane, Misquamicut, Rhode Island, 1938

The Distance of Trouble

Sitting under lunchroom tables
for the once-a-week air raid drill,
she wonders if this time
bombs will drop and blow them away—
her house, her family too. Or when,

late at night, more sirens,
but no Screaming "Meanies."
She looks out into the lamp-less night,
and prays Nazis are as far away as
the end of the alphabet with their V-1 rockets
and U-boats, or that her father,
dressed in his khaki Civilian Defense uniform,
carrying a billy club and flashlight,
will stop them. And are those sounds

of boots, tromping
leather-footed on the ground?
Finally, she hears the news—
Hitler has killed himself
in his underground fort.
She feels better until she sits

in a movie theater watching
a newsreel showing the bodies
of Mussolini and his mistress strung up
like the carcasses hanging behind
the counter in Charlie's Butcher Shop.
After that, when food shopping with her mother
she is even more afraid of Charlie and his big
blood-mottled white apron. She wonders

if the fanged men she's heard called "Japs"
wear the same kind of aprons when
they slaughter innocent babies; like the ones
she sees on roadside billboards—
their bellies slit open with blood-tipped knives.

She wonders how they eat with those large
buck teeth and where they are hiding, until
she hears a mushroom cloud
carried them away, and she sees the giant
heads of monster clouds on the front page
of her father's newspaper.

She isn't sure if these events
have anything to do with bodies
that look like burnt matchsticks,
which turned up at places with strange
names like Auschwitz and Buchenwald.

At summer camp, the year she is eight,
she wonders if the war will ever end
or just continue running alongside
her and all the other campers.
Then, one Sunday morning, a counselor
from Cabin One runs up the path
gasping, shrieking,
The war is over!
The Emperor has surrendered!
The war is over!

In this royal moment of relief,
as they dance, and jump, and hug,
she doesn't realize the world's grief
would catch up with them—sooner or later—
nor does she realize that war is never
going to run out of breath.

Now What Will We Do?

My panty-clad mother stands before
the ironing board, crying, wiping her eyes
with one hand, sawing the iron over shirts with the other.
She's drawn the drapes against the intense
summer heat. A shapeless light surrounds
her desire. My father has missed another promotion
from the bank. She waves the iron near her ear
as she shakes out another shirt.

Why can't he push himself, speak up?
Now what will we do? Now what will we do?

In the dining room I open my Bible coloring book,
select a black crayon and draw a handlebar
mustache on the face of Jesus.
Mother sets down her iron, advances on me
and snatches up my efforts.

Never deface the face of Jesus, never—
even atheists don't do such things!

She shakes me back and forth
as if to iron the devil out of me.
I thought, *Jesus wouldn't mind,*
he's as gentle as my father.

Whistling Girls and Cackling Hens Always Come to Some Bad End

One of my mother's frequent admonitions

If whistling girls might escape aprons
like my mother wore
and large breasts like Jane Russell's,
I thought I might practice more.

When I whistled, I pursed my lips
and tried to blow so forcefully
my breasts would never look like
the overblown pair
of Rita Hayworth's.

I whistled and whistled. Summers
I slipped into jeans,
went bare-chested,
rode horses on Uncle Hap's farm
where the sweet smell of hay,
like the horses themselves,
rushed out when the latch was lifted
and the barn door swung wide.
I galloped into a blaze
of restless fields of dandelions.

When I noticed swelling
behind my nipples,
I upped the volume of my whistling,
but Mother told me, finally,
I had to wear a shirt.
I still held out a stubborn hope
that when I grew up I'd be free
to ride by mountain streams
where water rushed and changed, but
like me, kept its own sounds, its own shape.

Sandy (left) and best friend Anne King,
both 9 years old, at Uncle Hap's farm
near Princeton, New Jersey, 1946

A Wood Bordered My Childhood Home

At the last high school reunion
a classmate asked,
Did you have a happy childhood?

In this dimming day, the question returns.
The rule-bound years? *Turn off the lamp?*
Kneel for your prayers?

Yes, of course, for no one was really watching,
and the footsteps in the hall
were never those of Jesus,

and you were free in a world of no particular country.
In those days, you appointed yourself
a guardian of trees.

From your bedroom window you kept an eye on
the tree house—all its furniture
constructed with branches

and moveable stones. In those days
you didn't always
have to be human.

Look back as if you were
in those maples and birches, as if
you were in that window of believing.

Turn to what can still be learned—
of woods, words,
and wind that bent there.

Martin and I first became friends in kindergarten
sitting under a cafeteria table during air raid drills,
or as we filled Red Cross boxes with toothpaste,
towels, and washcloths for our soldiers.

When we were thirteen, Gene Kelly,
that American in Paris, kissed Leslie Caron,
and for the first time I got the same thrill,
but not from Martin.

In our seventeenth year, Marilyn Monroe married
my hero, Joe DiMaggio, and I started going steady
with our high school quarterback, Jack Cuozzo,
while Martin sat on the porch and talked with my father.

When we graduated in 1955, Korea was still divided.
Martin shipped out across the Pacific to guard
the 38th parallel, sending back a cascade
of letters about rifles, flies, and missing me.

My distant relationship with Martin became more
complicated as had Marilyn Monroe's marriage,
now to Arthur Miller. We were twenty when
Martin returned and for our first formal date

he brought me a gardenia corsage, a passionate kiss,
and a proposal: *I will wait a long time,*
but not forever. America took its first
casualty in Vietnam that fall of 1957.

1980, not long after Carter's failed attempt to free
the hostages in Iran, I learned, as I packed
for our 25th high school reunion, Martin
had died from cancer. I didn't make the trip.

Twenty-five years later, George W. Bush was
re-elected, and that spring I went to my 50th.
Divorced for 20 years, I was ready for relief,
but whose idea was it that we revisit

Eagle Rock? From this old lovers' lane
on this mountaintop we could gaze
across the Hudson River and see
the distant outline of New York City,

now missing the Twin Towers.
Later, under the strobe lights, surrounded by
rock and roll music, Jack, the quarterback,
asked me to dance. I didn't have the heart.

I drove back up to Eagle Rock, sat in the dark
and talked to Martin. It was as warm as the summer
evening he was outside my window when Father
strode across my bedroom rug, leaned out

the open window and said, sternly
into the growing dark, *Go home, Martin.*
Gandhi had been assassinated earlier that year.
We were eleven years old. It was 9:00 pm.

2

Life and Death Matters

1937

Roosevelt Townes and Robert McDaniels
got no pity. Their story
and thousands like it, buried by indifference.

How an angry mob of white men seized them
from the sheriff and chained each to a tree
in Duck Hill, Mississippi. How five hundred

white men, women, and children gathered
to witness the blue-white flames of blowtorches
burn the skin off their backs

while they were questioned about their sins,
How that mob laughed as the men screamed.

Eventually, the instigators shot McDaniels then
lit a dry-brush pyre drenched in gasoline around
Townes, consuming him in flames.

In the North, just three months before, my mother
had parted her legs and struggled to deliver me
into waiting hands of love,

while the tattered world of white sheets
and its bloody mobs
guarded its restless borders

and the world waited for me, for my cohorts,
to grow up, change the sheets, change
history, to wipe away the stain.

In a More Privileged Place I

1937–1955
  Nana and Awah's House, 15 Parkway, Upper Montclair, New Jersey

A sharp buzz sounded in the kitchen
sending Blanche out through the pantry
into the dining room. Nana had pressed

a button under the dining room table summoning
Blanche for instruction, who then would disappear,
returning with entrees for answers

surrounded by porcelain plates and heavy silverware,
always in her eyelet-trimmed white apron
and green maid's uniform that reminded

me, Nana's granddaughter, of spinach.
Before dessert, I would escape
to the kitchen to help Blanche with the undressing

of dinner plates. I would take this time alone
with her to ask why girls were always in the kitchen
and boys, such bullies at school, were not.

Miz Sanny Jane, swiping at the wisps
of her hair graying at her forehead,

Mercy, mercy, she would exclaim,
seeing this girl standing there
in a happy place, complaining.

*Miz Sanny Jane, ain't you got
no worries bigger than that
to cry 'bout, girl?*

I would carry the silver pitcher to refill
water glasses, trying not to spill out questions,
but later, I asked my mother why we couldn't

invite Blanche to dinner at our house.
Mother was silent.
So what's wrong with Negroes?

Nana replied, *Blanche is not like the others,*
she knows her place.

On Sundays, with her brown hands floured
to knead the dough, Blanche pressed down hard.
She cracked the eggs just so,

and scrambled her obligations into small clumps.
I took them for love from Blanche
who I thought of as my *sideways* grandmother.

But where does she go by bus?
When does she go to church
if she comes here on Sunday?

Who takes care of her children
while she is taking care of us?
Does she have a husband?

These questions and their answers left each night
with Blanche on her homeward bus to Newark.

Blanche Rice,
15 Parkway, Upper Montclair, New Jersey
Home of Sandra's grandparents, Charles and Bessie Newmiller
circa 1929

Skating Away

The creek next to Nana and Awah's meandered
to a pond. In winter it froze as still
as I was listening to my father read
a story about Hans Brinker, a young boy
who skated on icy canals lacing
the land of Haarlem, Holland. *No this was not
Harlem, New York, but a land far away*.

On wintry days when I stayed
with my grandparents, I often imagined
Hans gliding up and down the creek's smooth
surface, wooden skates strapped to his shoes.

I would sling my skates over my shoulder,
trudge to the park and put them on
in front of the skating hut's coal-glowing,
wrought-iron stove. I'd study
the shining metal blades
attached to my white leather boots.

My father had explained that for poor Hans,
metal blades like mine were unaffordable—
most likely as precious as silver.
As I pulled on my bulky woolen socks,
I thought, some things seemed better
the less you know about them.

Once out on the ice I could look down
at my reflection, seeing the floating clouds above,
hoping to glide somewhere beyond New Jersey.
Maybe go as far away as Holland,
meet Hans, his family, and friends.

When I sensed my toes were red
as wrinkled beets, I donned my snow boots,
left the mirrored lake,
and returned to my grandmother's kitchen.
Blanche was sure to be there, hot cocoa ready,
a wisp of smoke curling from the cup.

Blanche had never read *Hans Brinker*
or the Silver Skates, but she was happy
to hear the story and agreed
sure 'nough that Hans—such a hard worker—
helpin' his sister with gettin' new skates.
Mercy, mercy, instead he had to use that money
to pay them doctor bills for his father.

And she added, *and I didn't grow up*
near no ponds that froze. *Mercy, mercy,*
I didn't have no time to skate,
too much work to do. Mercy, mercy,
too much work to do.

In a More Privileged Place II

1952–1955
Hoboken, New Jersey

This *sideways* granddaughter remembers
tattered flags of laundry flapping
atop tenement roofs as if appealing
for a truce. I watched through

the Erie Lackawanna's dusty windows
on my way to the city, on my way
to Wednesday dance lessons, or to visit
my father's Wall Street office. I wondered

about this different world, remembered
the day an edition of *Life* magazine lay open
on the living room coffee table at home,
its cover advertising a photo essay on poverty.

Here were the people pinning laundry
to those clotheslines. Here they were, sitting
in ragged shorts at a table listing
on its broken legs. Sagging wallpaper,

a backdrop to the scene; a bare bulb
overhead sending angry electricity
to the edge of the page. They had dark faces.
A boy about my age staring straight

into what seems to be nothing
and I looked, too,
but couldn't see the answer.
On Sunday evenings,

the lights turned out, as instructed,
I would dial my transistor radio
to gospel music broadcast from churches
in a place called Harlem.

My ancestors once lived there.
Now, from a more privileged place
I promised to *change the world someday*—
a promise I made to the night.

A Wider World Comes Into View

1955

August

    I arrive at a hilltop college campus overlooking Long Island Sound; not exactly a Homeric tale, but a journey, books in my head and in my hands, an odyssey of my own. I never thought much about what was to come, even though a thread of violence weaves through most of history. Just as I was leaving for school, terrible news breaks into headlines. This is the 1950s, white-robed ghosts with peaked hoods are on the rise again in the South, wreaking havoc as they go. *A fourteen-year-old boy Emmett Till, abducted from his uncle's home in Money, Mississippi, in the middle of the night, has been found. His mutilated body surfaced from the Tallahatchie River.* His mother insisted his savaged body with his mangled face be laid out in an open casket at Robert's Temple of God, Chicago, a testament for all to see. I saw the pictures. One eye out of its socket—it hangs in my mind with the one-eyed Cyclops, as described by Odysseus, prompting me to conjure the screams heard by someone near the river the night of the murder. Testimony from the trial of the murderers: that Emmett cried out *Mother* as he was tortured, his facial bones broken. He was found with barbed wire wrapped around his neck and around the seventy-five pound metal fan used to sink him in the river, drowning any mythology that in a post-slavery world Negroes were faring any better a century after being set free. And regardless of the patronizing kindness many friends and relatives of mine and the rest of the white world might show, the murderous consequences of this misshapen view were as lethal in the '50s as they had been the three preceding centuries.

December

    Walking the snow-dusted campus of Connecticut College in early winter, the horizon of Long Island Sound is surrounded with fog, fog as thick as the prospects for civil rights success of Negroes organizing in the South. I was unaware then that in Alabama the story of Emmet Till was seen through a sharper lens. Rosa Parks, a civil rights activist, was further infuriated by Emmet's fate and the lack of care by the authorities for the lives of Negroes. As we now know, on December 1, Miss Parks was seated in the front row of the "colored" section at the back of a bus in Birmingham, Alabama. The bus filled with white people, so driver James F. Blake, himself white, asked the three "coloreds" and Miss Parks to stand, thus making room for more whites to sit. *Y'all better make it light on yourselves and let me have these seats.* Three got up, Miss Parks did not. She was marched off to jail in her cloth coat and brimless hat. The next news I heard was that all the buses leaving Birmingham and its outer rings were empty of Negroes, none willing to sit in the back of buses as instructed. They began walking into a new story. I was elated. I wondered what Blanche thought of this, but I was sure she wouldn't mention it to Nana, nor would Nana, if she noticed, talk to Blanche about it. And I didn't mention it to either one.

What Was Unearthed Today

When we return, we will show you pictures of the crime scene.
I'm warning you these pictures are disturbing. And I will tell you
about the autopsy report that we received from an anonymous source,
which notes that Andrew Goodman had fragments of clay in his lungs
and chunks of clay held in his fists, so even though shot in the heart
the report indicates he was buried alive.
—Walter Cronkite, CBS Evening News, *September 1, 1964*

The sun through the high windows
falls on my eleventh-grade classmates,
a light breeze sets the shades flapping.
Miss Grimes is discussing the 1870
ratification of the Fifteenth Amendment
to the US Constitution, the right to vote
not to be denied to citizens
because of race. How wonderful,
I think—allowing, finally,
former slaves to vote, an example
for all the world to see
America in 1955.

Almost a decade later, I've learned
more about the disastrous period after
the Civil War when former slaves
suffered continued violence and were denied
the vote for the century to come.

Freedom Summer is in full swing
upending this despotism, a growing outcry
rises throughout the land to help organize
the southern struggle. Northerners,

both Black and white, pitch in.
It is June and three Freedom Riders
are missing. As summer ends, burnt-out
expectations are confirmed when their charred
station wagon is discovered, and their bodies
dug out of an earthen dam
on a Ku Klux Klansman's farm.

    Andrew Goodman.
    Michael Schwerner.
    James Chaney.

Murdered. And six more bodies recovered,
unknown black children and black men,
exhumed in other places during the search.

With three small sons and a husband
I can't hop a bus, head south to become
a Freedom Rider or march with Martin
Luther King toward his dream as much as I
want to. But I can send a few dollars

to him, to the ACLU. I can talk
to friends. and commiserate with my minister,
Gene Bridges, on the beating death
of his friend, Reverend James Reeb,
after they marched together in Selma.
And I promise to raise my three sons
to work against violence and divisiveness.

I think back on the innocence
of my teen-age bravado, and how
Miss Grimes and others never saw
that they portrayed US history
as a tale of white people, excluding
the country's indigenous people
and those brought here in slave ships.

We have to unwind the past, face the truth.
and write an inclusionary future.
If we don't, we will sit here tomorrow—
like today—with this clay in our mouths.
Yes, this clay in our mouths.

The Insufferable Summer of Urban Riots
with the War Dead Continuing to Return Home

1967
    Fort Carson, Colorado

After two years of residency at Tripler Army Hospital, my husband withdrew from the program. Now he owed the Army two more years of service as payback, but since he was studying to become a pathologist rather than a surgeon, the powers that be didn't send him to Vietnam, instead reassigned him in 1966 to a hospital lab at Fort Carson, Colorado. Meanwhile my parents, still living in my childhood home in New Jersey, came for a visit, once we settled in. The US was far from settled; not only was the war in Indochina a total killing field, the nation's newspapers, its TV channels were filled with details and images of riots breaking out everywhere in American cities: Atlanta, Boston, Cincinnati, Buffalo, Tampa, Milwaukee, Detroit, and, worst of all—Newark, New Jersey. The disappointments of the civil rights movements, the dire situation of Blacks in the major cities, and in the war, these injustices were rubbed raw by the end of the '60s. The images of police brutality lit the flames, especially the Los Angeles police abuse of Rodney King.

There was nothing but a huge red glow over the entire city of Newark, the city in flames—a war zone. Buildings were smashed, windows, broken. You saw a very angry crowd, and they saw you.
    Paul Zigo, member of the New Jersey National Guard
        New York Times, July 17, 1967

Although the city appeared to be returning to normal, there was yet another fatal incident early today. A negro was shot and killed by police in the negro section while allegedly attempting to loot a store. His death was the 26th since the rioting began Wednesday.
        New York Times, July 17, 1967

My father and I are watching the chaos of the streets, flames flashing across our TV screen. Finally, he burst out, almost shouting:

It's terrible, terrible, all these riots. Look what's going on in right next to us in Newark. A place our law-abiding relatives have lived for years. They are destroying property, hurting innocent people, burning everything in sight. Animals, I say, animals! Send them all back to Africa!

Dad, Dad, don't say that!

It's unimaginable! It's unforgivable!

Remember after WW II, those African American soldiers returning home who were lynched instead of being welcomed and that after risking their lives for this country? Maybe I hadn't told you our African American neighbor, an Army major, came home this month in a body bag from Vietnam? So if you are a true American, what war did you fight in?

Well, I am sorry about your neighbor, but destroying property, and violently flouting the police isn't right.

My dad, born in 1905, can't seem to see beyond the flames, beyond the tree-lined streets of his own (and once mine) serene white neighborhood. Nor, sadly, can he undo what he learned in school—the slaves weren't smart enough for equal freedom or equal opportunity. We sat on the couch, turned off the CBS *Evening News*—no end to 400 years of strife. The TV images flicker and die.

Blanche's face flashed through my mind. Was she still alive? Would she think of this cauldron of conflict with pride in resistance or sorrow?

Dear Blanche,

I'm so sorry you and I lost touch. Are you still alive? Blanche, I wish there were some way I could have talked to you about race. So confusing as a child. Jesus taught me one thing while those around me seemed to think another. "Oh she gets upset about so many things, just too sensitive," my mother said of me. Skin color seemed to matter. Yes, treat everyone kindly, but keep in mind, Black people are not quite as smart and need to be watched a little more carefully.

It is hard to live in a world still separated into Black and white, rich and poor.

Luckily, it's a bit different now. I am in graduate school at the University of Maryland School of Social work and interning at the Maryland Human Rights Commission here in Baltimore. Thankfully, some friends I've made in graduate school and at the Commission are Black. I am one of three white people in the Commission office. I have learned not only from my colleagues, but also from seeing the problems minorities face daily. I realize there is so much I don't think about, haven't experienced. Back at the School of Social Work, I am fortunate to be in a special program with about forty students; many are African Americans, so a mix of white and Black students will often get together, especially after our community organizing classes, and have endless discussions about race and racism. It may sound funny to say this, but, Blanche, it is as if I finally got a chance to talk to your grandchildren, not just the children of my parents' friends all of whom were, of course, white.

At school talking about how I feel the pain of racism—the guilt, brought expected blowback toward me, as the Black students pointed out it was never a life or death issue for me. I would never be strung up, or ever likely to be shot or beat up by the police.

I think I got the right advice when my classmates told me, don't worry about us, just work with white people, try to free them from their delusions. *You sit at the table with whites—You hold that power, baby.* That was inspiring, but what was most painful when an African American colleague I was closest to said one night: *You might think we are fighting the same fight, but you can go home, you can leave us. We can never leave the scene. We are here permanently, no choice. Yes, you can be my friend, but my sist*er? *No, not yet.* I know, Blanche, this country's history of shame cannot just be washed away. All I can do is work on it.

Well, my fantasy letter is done, since I can't talk to you any more. When I was little, after you listened to me complain about something, you'd place your arms akimbo, tilt your head, look at me, and ask me this question: *Ain't you got anything else more important to worry about, girl?* And this question to this day absolutely dismounts me from my high horse. I don't think I'm riding one now, but I'm glad I put this all down, and regardless of its inadequacy, I just want to say thank you, and please forgive me for all I might and should have done, given your good examples, much earlier in life.

Love,
Sandy (I go by this now).

Roots: Found Poem Written After Reading the Narrative of a Former Slave's Experience

My massa was a killer.
He got in trouble there in Georgia and got him
two good-stepping hosses
    and the covered wagon.
Then he chains all he slaves round the necks
fastens the chains to the hosses
makes them walk all the way to Texas.
Somewhere on the road
    it went to snowin',
and Massa wouldn't let us wrap anything
round our feet. We had to sleep on the ground
in all the snow. Massa have a great,
long whip out of rawhide,
and when one the niggers fall behind or give out,
he hit him with that whip.
    It take the hide every time
he hit a nigger. Mother, she give out
on the way, 'bout the line of Texas.
Her feet got raw and bleedin' and her legs swoll
    plumb out of shape.
Then Massa, he jus' take out he gun
and shot her, and whilst she lay dying'
he kicks her two, three times and say,
    Damn a nigger
        what can't stand nothin'.
Jus' leave her layin' where he shot her at.

Ben Simpson, former slave, age 90,
Madisonville, Texas

Upon the Occasion of the United States Congress Passing a Resolution in 2005 Apologizing for Having Done Nothing to Prevent the 4,742 Lynchings After the Civil War

Whereas history books tell us this Black person
and that Black person died swinging from a tree,
or that one, dangling from a bridge;

Whereas bodies buried in shallow graves,
once dug up give no clues,
nor can anyone report who was who;

Whereas regrets alone have no benefits
for the beloved of the deceased,
the living, or the not yet born;

Whereas all the ancestors who once swung
in the breeze, sway to the currents of today—
we are still buffeted by their troubled spirits—

Be it resolved we who are troubled spirits too,
will commit ourselves anew
to affirming the sacred life of everyone.

After Layli Long Soldier

In a Carceral State

October 2010
Natchez, Mississippi

On the first day of our tour, I witness
the city's unscathed antebellum splendor.
We travel past banks with temple-like facades,
massive churches, and one large gray marble
synagogue. We enter The First Presbyterian
where under the stained-glass light of Jesus

we absorb our guide's tales of the halcyon days
of slave-picked cotton, the marvels of the cotton gin,
and the generous investments of Northern
bankers; everyone harboring glorious
expectations that cotton sales would build
Natchez into the New York of the South.

On the second day, we bend our heads under
old oaks draped in Spanish moss to step through
the front door of an eighteenth-century mansion,
enter its parlor filled with polished mahogany furniture,
floral drapes, slipcovers, satin lampshades
and relics from the family's slave-owning past.

My discomfort stems not only from this setting
and the straight-backed chair I sit in, but
the gaze I sense of someone behind me. I turn
to see a dark oil painting hung above the mantel piece,
a portrait of a young woman, her peach-colored skin
displayed by her off-shoulder ball gown.

She is staring at me. Her eyes have a desperate
glow, as if pleading with me, someone
to set her free from the confinement
of her station, as if desperate to shake off
the oppression she continually witnesses,
but is unable to change.

I glance at my fellow travelers—do they
feel this connection? She hangs, caught
in this history as am I, as we all are.
I feel a bond with her suffering. How do you
change when you belong to a privileged class
that is doing so much you despise?

I want to believe my instincts are not false.
In any evil system, many don't sympathize,
yet have little power to tear down
what their privileged class constructs.
So few seem able to free their own
societies, to make the needed corrections.

I want to I tell her how far we've moved on
since the Civil War, but I have only the blues
men's songs, tales of heroic feats
of the great migration North,
and the semi-successful struggles
of the civil rights movement of the 1960s.

I haven't lost hope. *Hang in there,*
I whisper. We can't redeem or redraw
the past, but I think we have a chance
to wipe off some of the old oil, craft
a better future in the much brighter colors
so many of us have imagined.

3

Grandparents Awah and Nana
(Charles and Bessie Newmiller)
in their living room at 15 Parkway,
beside Sandy's picture circa 1945

A Visit to 15 Parkway, Upper Montclair, New Jersey

> *No one spoke,*
> *The host, the guest,*
> *The white chrysanthemums.*
>   *—Ryota*

Through the French doors
    out in the garden
        behind the house on Parkway,
I see you, Awah,
    bending down,
        the white New Jersey noon
heavy on your back
    as you clip your favorite roses.

Across quiet oriental rugs
    I find you, Nana,
        sitting in the soft light
of your living room writing
    at the maple secretary,
        your back to me.

A single rose stands
    on a thin crystal leg
        to keep us company.

The clock ticks
    on the mantel,
        china dogs stare down
from the bookcase,
    mute,
        as this grandchild watches.

And, Blanche,
    you are busy in the kitchen,
        burnishing the pots
and pans, talking to me,
    sunlight streaking the window.

I see now the landscape
    of our lives,
        the enclosure of your plans,

but I would need
    enormous language, Nana,
        to have you turn to me,
    for you, Awah,
        to bring me roses,
and for you, Blanche,
    to reassure me that one day
        we would all understand.

Eleanor, age 6, and her father, Anthony Wills, age 36,
Summer 1914

What Usually Is Seen as too Small to Mention

For Natalie Katerina Larson, my granddaughter, and in memory
of Anthony Charles Wills (her second great-grandfather) and
Eleanor Wills Newmiller Sidman (her great-grandmother)

On readying my mother's dollhouse for my granddaughter,
this daughterless mother picks up the plot.

A gift to my mother, the dollhouse was crafted
by her father for the Christmas of her seventh year.

Delighted with it, she was setting up housekeeping
the day after Christmas, naming the dolls, rearranging the chairs

when the news came her father, age thirty-six, had dropped dead
on New York City's Cortland Street while looking in a storefront window.

I, who never met this grandfather, or knew he had existed,
was shocked at age eleven when my mother finally told me this story.

She never explained how she rearranged her grief
to accept a stepfather and a stepsister, or how she continued

to organize her small household, or what she told the dolls.
In this world of miniature size, she managed well enough

to thrive, or so it seemed, well enough to preserve these porcelain
dolls and their home for me. So here they are, this family:

Mother, with perfectly organized hair constantly keeps straightening
the household for the return of faithful father.

The family stares at little silver forks, knives and spoons as correctly set
as the evening's conversation. In the kitchen the refrigerator keeps

everything fresh without a chill. The Campbell soup can, unopened,
remains on the pantry shelf where once again the catsup doesn't spill.

Through a kitchen door swung wide, the maid brings in
the evening meal, a roast cemented to its platter, tiny potatoes by its side.

In the living room fireplace, grated coals emit a steady glow
as father tries to retrieve his favorite novel anchored to the bookshelf.

Mother and father talk a while before sleep, until the dollhouse-keeper
securely latches the outer walls, and turns off the porch light.

As I am sure my mother did, I wish
them all good night, hoping my granddaughter

will use this gift from her great-great-grandfather,
her great-grandmother, and me

to hold in place these spaces of love.

Three Newmiller women in the living room at 15 Parkway
Isabelle, Bessie (Nana), and Eleanor (Sandy's mother)
circa 1923

Dear Aunt Isabelle

*In memory of Isabelle Ann (Newmiller) West
June 17, 1915–September 5, 1956*

I was eighteen that September they found you, crumpled
on your bathroom floor. You slipped,
they said. You died. You were only forty-one.

In the dim-lit funeral parlor my cousin Dorothy
ran to your open coffin, demanding that you *Get Up*!
and love her. I needed you to do the same for me.
In this parlor of grief, memories rush toward me:

of holidays that often began with you whirling
into the living room, my three younger cousins
and Uncle Alan in tow; your wink as you passed
the forbidden olives under the table, after
I had been told I was not old enough to eat them;
how delighted I was when you threw the left-over spinach
out the kitchen window, because Blanche,
jokingly, told you that was the best place for it.

After dinner on those overstuffed holidays, you might
break into a skinny-legged Charleston, while your father,
Awah, sat in his wing-backed chair smiling at your antics,
ringed by pipe smoke, a scent I still recognize. Or
one afternoon, when Nana and Mother were absorbed
in the merits of wallpaper samples stabbed to the living room wall,
you stood behind them rolling your eyes, your arms flailing,
as if this was a game of charades for me and Awah to enjoy.
Your laugh was bigger than you were, as if you inhaled it
from his pipe smoke and let it out every time he told a joke.

I was eleven years old when Mother told me
she was eleven when your widowed father married
her widowed mother and brought you home
to this newly knitted family. A step-sister. You screamed
my mother said. Eventually everyone's grief
was stored away, routine set in. Perhaps
this is the root of my reflection—

there is often a flimsiness to silence. When life
forces you to substitute one mother for another,
you come to realize that wherever you stand
you must choose what is important for yourself.
You, the youngest in the family were a steppingstone
to my mother and Nana. You loosened
some of the strait-laced admonitions that flourished there.

Dear Aunt Isabelle, you were like Peter Pan on a theatrical wire,
you gave me confidence to seek a different path. I left
for college and a new life. You were always with me—
urging me to fly.

On Holding an Amethyst

In memory of Eleanor Farrington (Wills/Newmiller) Sidman
November 22, 1907–June 5, 1988

As a mother you had many facets,
only some could I touch,
those other edges were for my father.

As time passed, I realized you once
had a larger shape. As a girl
and a young woman, edges were polished
away. You could be comforting
to the touch. You could envelope me,

though your inner light was not easy
to penetrate. Now that you are gone
I form your memory into a shape
I can hold in my hand,
imagining the light and color
of our history, and here is what
I want to say:

With all the time
that has crystallized,
you are still
beautiful to me and I feel
your elemental strengths vein
the color of my soul.
Because for you to be my mother,
you chose to let light in.

Eleanor Newmiller (Sandy's mother) in Rhode Island circa 1929

Dad, Who's to Know What Will Happen Next?

In memory of A. Gordon Sidman, Jr.
May 24, 1905–July 10, 1991

Deerfield Beach, Florida

In your house I am surrounded
by sundials, thermostats, rain gauges, light
timers, and time
pieces that tick. Mostly, Dad,
you did careful things—
turned off the hot water valves
after each bath, unplugged
the toaster and TV, had more than enough
smoke alarms, installed triple locks
on all the doors and embedded
water sprinklers near your fruit trees.

You always paid your bills, scheduled
the gardener weeks in advance, topped off
a full tank of gas, kept everything mechanical
oiled, wrote detailed notes
in your datebook—but today's page

is blank. Water nozzles drip
as I stand in a sea of smoldering
sockets, and the Oldsmobile's tires are flat,
and the sundial shadow doesn't move
as I go out into your garden to touch
the grapefruit and mango trees hanging
with fruit. *Mr. Sidman has died*, I tell them.

They are wild with grief,
wild with grief.

Sandy dancing with her father, Gordon Sidman,
on the night of her son's wedding, June 15, 1991

Dandelions

2021
Evergreen Cemetery, Brooklyn, New York

Seated below high blue,
I loved to surround myself
with dandelions raising
their golden heads
in my field of clover and grass.
As a young girl I would sit alone,
breathing in silence,
breathing in peace.

An old woman now, I stand
below huge oak trees
in a vast cemetery;
the white architecture
of remembrance popping up
over acres of dying grass.

Finally, I've found the plots
of generations of my mother's
ancestors—babies who did not live
long enough to sit in highchairs,
young wives lost in childbirth,
teenagers wedded to the earth
instead of a fertile marriage bed,
and the aged laid wearily to rest.

Breathe in silence.
Breathe in peace. Yes,
they are here, beneath the turf,
the cemetery official claims,
all fifteen or more,
but where are the headstones?

Were they never erected or
couldn't the families afford them?
Were they blown over, removed?
No. Headstones are not dandelions.

Just as well I brought no bouquet.
No place to put them. Memories
of the past, where do they dwell?
Yet I did come to tell them of the future
they didn't live to see, to mingle
our lives, our dreams.

As the October sun begins to turn
oaks and their golden leaves
into a temple of burnished memory,
I leave this place of the past
thinking of the girl among the clover—
she is gone as are all her older relatives,
like the dandelions in the field—
and now too, she awaits the wind.

4

Four Children in the Picture

*"Harriet Tubman Series #4" by Jacob Lawrence
displayed at the Minneapolis Institute of Art*

But yet this leap of hope—
these handstands

of early morning joy.
No note of oppression's bitter salt,

freedom that feels like
a somersault over pebbles

in the sand. The sky,
mute above the four,

the back flip of a boy,
and there are millions more;

to our shame,
fleeing equal pain

that hoped, that jumped
that wanted to cartwheel

into a more welcoming world.
Do we ever apologize?

How ridiculous you say, but
I have seen these children living

in this museum—their world curated
but never corrected.

A Child's Welfare

1

Where I come from forsythia bloom
in April. Tulips
were satin to my eyes.

Mother said,
Look.
Don't touch.

Lilacs and lilies perfumed the air at Easter.
My sailor coat covered an organza dress.
My hat bounced in the pew.

Quiet, whispered Father, *sit still.*
Be like the lilies lining the aisle.

2

No lilacs or lilies decorate these days
at Easter when I go riding with Julia,
a foster child who wants to pick

flowers for her mother, wandering
somewhere among shards
of old wine glasses. And gone too,

her father—last seen driving off
in an old pick-up truck.
She is left

with a half-brother with sores on his butt
because urine is acid to the skin of a child
who hasn't been changed for a while.

And she was forced to open too soon to a father
who heard no voice from the past:
Look, but don't touch.

And no one to tell her not to touch flowers
or to sit still in the face of good news,
so I must gather her in as my own.

I want to march down the aisle and to all
the congregation say, *Speak, it is that time of year.*
Hold lilacs and lilies, I say, but speak
for the children. Speak.

Tommy

I don't like ... the curtains.

Ah, I bet in time they could be changed.
What do you think of Mike and Jane?
They'd like to become your parents.

OK, I guess, but why
won't my foster parents keep me?

How do you tell an eight-year-old boy
he might be lucky we've found
a childless couple that wants him as a son
regardless of whether he will love them in return.

As Tommy and I drive through the neighborhood
back to his foster home, he has another question.

Can't I stay with you?

The elm trees look
tired, ready to forget
about shielding us from the summer sun.

No, Tommy, my job is to find you
a home. Plus, I'm moving out of town.

I don't tell him he lives in a society that doesn't value
vulnerable children enough to provide birth
parents with the help needed to keep them.
We talk about curtains and other things.
By our next visit, Jane has changed them.

I don't recall the intervening paperwork, the numerous visits,
but I remember the brightly colored cars and trucks
traveling over the linen lanes printed on the curtain fabric,

and the small backyard in which Mike gave Tommy
a baseball glove, where they began the back and forth
of lofting trust in this new world of a father-son relationship.

2

Highways took me away from this story, left me
wondering if the next social worker was monitoring
the outward signs of this family's bonding.

No longer in those hallways of meager help,
my calculations tell me Tommy now would be
in his late sixties.

I wonder whether he is father to children, tossed
balls back and forth with his kids, even grandkids,
whether he liked his work, loved his partner,
whether he learned to love himself.

Sometimes in a fabric store as I browse
through the bolts of cloth suitable for curtains,
I wonder if those cars and trucks carried
the love he needed for the long haul.

Really?

In the early 1960s, when I was a child protection worker for the Ramsey County, Minnesota, Welfare Department, I was the proud owner of an exceptional vehicle. My teenage male clients—all wards of the State—loved riding in it with me, no matter where I was taking them. *Can I drive, oh please, please? No, no, you aren't old enough yet—maybe someday you too can have a car like this.* It was a 1939 Oldsmobile. Under the hood a silver-painted '52 Ford truck engine with dual carburetors to match and a green exterior with red flames flickering over both flanks of the car. There were other opinions about the car, however. One day my supervisor called me into her office, told me that the powers-that-be thought it unprofessional for me to be driving such a hot rod. I nodded and rode on anyway. It was clear to me that "the powers that be" didn't have a firm grasp on our supposed mission—heading all the children under our protection toward a brighter, much classier future.

Welfare cuts come under fire

By **Julie M. Gravelle**

Minneapolis United Way agencies have joined growing opposition to the proposed state welfare cuts being considered by the Legislature.

Directors of 40 of the 107 United Way agencies appeared at a news conference at the Minneapolis United Way headquarters Tuesday, announcing their opposition to the cuts, particularly in Aid to Families with Dependent Children benefits. All 107 agency heads voted last Friday to lobby against the cuts, marking the first time United Way agencies have banded together to oppose state cuts.

This week the House will vote on a proposed 30 percent—or $35 million—cut to the state's fund for AFDC.

Agencies protesting the proposed cuts include Catholic Charities of St. Paul and Minneapolis, Minneapolis Urban League, Salvation Army, Greater Minneapolis Food Bank, YMCA and YWCA, Sabathani Community Center, Youth Emergency Services and the Legal Aid Society of Minneapolis.

They join several other groups and individuals, including Mayor Donald Fraser and Archbishop John Roach, who have spoken out against the cuts since they were proposed a week ago.

"This is the first time in the twenty-five year history of the Minneapolis Council of Agency Executives that we have taken such joint action," said Sandra Larson, president of the Minneapolis Council of Agency Directors. "We believe this issue is that important."

Mary Pat Brigger, executive director of the Domestic Abuse Project, said that most people on welfare, including children, mothers and the disabled, face tremendous barriers to employment and that funds to

Sandra Larson, chairman of the Council of Agency Executives, spoke Tuesday on behalf of 40 social service agency directors in denouncing the state's proposal to cut the AFDC budget by 30 percent.

Photo/Jeff Christensen

help them find work are also being pared down.

"What's happening now is happening to our clients, not just the programs," Brigger said.

Larson conceded that it is a "foregone conclusion" that the proposed 30 percent cut will pass the House this week. Instead, she said the agency directors will urge state senators to protest the cuts along with them.

Larson said the Minneapolis United Way agencies will be represented at a rally protesting AFDC cuts scheduled for Thursday at the State Capitol.

Minnesota Daily Press, February 26, 1986

The Absence of Help

Memo:

Baby ███████ is to be taken tomorrow into our custody because of the mother's criminal record, her severe drinking habits, the evidence of neglect such as the sores on the baby's bottom caused by the acidic build up from unchanged diapers.

Ramsey County Welfare Department, St. Paul, Minnesota, 1960

Location:

Selby Avenue, St. Paul, Minnesota

Incident report:

You've brung these cops with you, I see. If you didn't bring 'em, I'd have beat you to a bloody pulp.

(Of course you would, of course you would, and I'm not sure I'd blame you if it were my baby.)

Yes, sadly, the cops are necessary, Mrs. ████████████ *I understand how upset you are, but you have not lived up to caring for this baby girl. Look at these open wounds.*

(I know a mother's heart can have holes in it too. And what mother is redeemable?)

5

Dinner at the Edge of the Empire

1964
Honolulu, Hawaii

Guests of Dr. & Mrs. Wang: My husband and I,
and other Tripler Army Hospital doctors, medics, wives &
friends of the hosts, along with a contingent of Green Berets

A large all-American turkey, belly glistening, lies
in its crisp brown skin next to mounds
of scarlet cranberry sauce. The conversation

ricochets around the Berets—Vietnam:
    Where is that? What's the mission?
Also on the dining room table sit Ming-decorated

tureens of steaming rice, noodles tangled
in brown sauce, shiitake mushrooms buried
in them. The Berets talk of the mountain people,

the Montagnards. We learn their mission
is to train these "Yards" in guerilla warfare
to aid the faltering South Vietnamese.

The soldiers talk of the bad odds even if
there were more of them, even if they were to stay
in that green, humid, deadly place.

Mouths muffled with a full buffet,
advice falls like rice to the floor.
    We should stay out, stay out.
    The South Vietnamese shoot these hillbillies for sport.

Here comes the dim sum.
  Once we discovered a South Vietnamese jumping on the broken
  leg of a Yard after a war exercise failed.

  A mistake, a mistake to try and prop up
  the South Vietnamese against Ho Chi Minh's forces.

The hostess moves among the guests with a large silver tray
heaped with fortune cookies and their cryptic answers.

How many more soldiers will be sent to this war? The cookies
never mentioned millions.
          Numbers do not always sum
          to a happy outcome.

Doesn't the US have the power to win this war if we want to?
We unfold the next small slip of paper:
          Flowers only bloom
          from intrinsic strength.

Looking back on the decades of fighting yet to come,
the millions dead, no fortune cookie could know

what was blowing in the wind, although as I recall,
one small slip of paper had these words printed on it.
          Think beyond the unthinkable.

If the Impossible Were Possible

November 22, 1963

Let's imagine if bullets could trace back
into the gun barrel that rested
on the windowsill of the Texas School
Book Depository, and all that transpired
afterwards could be undone:
millions of massacred Cambodians,
Vietnamese, and Laotians would rise up
from blood-stained soil and return
to their villages; everyone caught
in the slaughter would go home,
their farms greening again and
their rice paddies growing fat;
never napalmed or withered
with Agent Orange, and children
would laugh and leap past
the uncontaminated ponds;
while body bags would open, soldiers,
would climb back into planes, whole again,
heading home to hugs from loved ones,
their arms filled with welcome leis.
And fall leaves crumpled at the base
of the granite reflecting wall on the Mall
in Washington D.C. would drift away,
as would all the visitors stroking
its shiny surfaces of loss, and
the Kennedys would return to riding through
a bright November day in Dallas,
Jackie's pillbox hat back on her head,

her strawberry wool bouclé suit worn anew
on the campaign trail, now that it is out
of its acid-free container, no longer bloody,
or stored away in a hidden place, and Jack
would be contemplating a dinner
with Martin Luther King to talk strategies
on how to defang all forms of hatred
toward "others," and the dream
would spread.

Seasons of Memory

Mother, all you remember is how you feel,
you don't remember anything.
         My son Andrew's complaint at age 16

I've read recently that medical researchers are working feverishly
to create pills to improve the memory. Would we really want
to dwell on the past—the loss of missing limbs,
old enemies, waiting rooms, burnt skin?

How would we appreciate the moment—a spring day
of cherry blossoms—if we were forced to live
in such a tenement of overcrowded memories?

My son Andrew was only five in 1968
when we visited the orthopedic clinic at Walter Reed
Army Hospital. We sat in the waiting room

with stacks of books to read, waiting for ghost pictures
of his femur and predictions about whether breaking it again
would spur growth in his one short leg.

All the other patients were men in blue and white seersucker robes
and army-issued slippers. I didn't ask Andrew what he thought
of them—those without their limbs, parts of their skulls blown in.

On our way home, we drove around the tidal basin,
huge marble buildings with the triumphal feel of Rome.
Cherry blossoms from Japan fringing everything.

I barely remember my mother's cousin who survived
the Bataan Death March and a Japanese prisoner-of-war camp.
Everyone is moving toward death, but marching there

was a different story, or so they said. He never spoke of it—
hundreds and hundreds of men dropping silently that spring.
Like a frail cherry blossom, once home, he didn't last.

The only bone I'd broken was my arm in a field at Camp Nyoda
as a girl. *Dearie, this is going to hurt.* One hand on my shoulder
and the other holding my wrist,

the doctor took the arm and yanked it
in that one perfect motion of realignment.
Phan Tri Kim Phúc, that little girl running down the road

trailing her burning skin, I read not long ago
that she is in Paris, and the green beauty of Vietnam
is bringing the tourists back again.

After the organizing, after the protests, I was home,
as I recall, each afternoon when the boys returned
from school. This year I've heard the cherry blossoms

are already blooming in Washington D.C.,
no tear gas, no police in plastic helmets
with mouth guards running toward us,

batons raised, or the thousands of protesters
on the mall. Now there is
just the honed granite wall.

And I have forgotten what the argument was about
or when Andrew first began to bring me flowers in spring.
Comfort is a complicated forgetting and remembering.

Imploding on the News While Reading T. S. Eliot's "The Wasteland"

January 17, 1991
Gulf War I

> *Here is not water, only rock.*
> *—T.S. Eliot*

Is Bush thinking
America can start "a new world order"?

> *What are you thinking of? What thinking? What?*
> *I never know what you are thinking. Think.*

At night I watch
the fiery hair of Baghdad

> *... her hair*

Spread out in fiery points
blowing up on my screen.

> *... Do*

> *You know nothing? Do you see nothing? Do you remember*
> *Nothing?*

Civilization's cradle rocking again.
It is difficult to track
our position in the sand.

> *I can connect*
> *Nothing with nothing*
> *The broken fingernails of dirty hands.*

We, of course, have the advantage, using
starlight for eyes.

> *Only at nightfall, aethereal rumours*

A *Mirage* jet fighter, speaking exquisite French, drops bombs
on men and boys conscripted to fry
in their makeshift bunker graves.

... so many,
I had not thought death had undone so many.

In my living room, I see the black crosses of range finders,
puffs of smoke, then the destruction.
Day by day I get the hollow blow-by-blow.
Our young men pawing like stallions.
   HURRY UP PLEASE ITS TIME.

Young Marines with only stubble on their heads
saying "I'm going out to bag me some Iraqi."
"Watching people drop, the ultimate game."
"This is the way the big boys play."

Relief maps, color-coded diagrams, big boy
generals, on TV, answer questions of anchormen,
talking heads with desert scenes behind them.
   Fishing, with the arid plains behind me
   Shall I at least set my lands in order?

I cannot untangle the algorithms.
Trapped here with only men's ideas,
I turn off the TV. Wild dogs.
   The wind under the door.

Words in italics are from T.S. Eliot's "The Wasteland"

Morning Witness

1995
  Lake Superior, Grand Marais, Minnesota

A young man stands frozen
in a city plaza for a moment,
 as if trying to decipher

what has just happened—
his neck sliced through
like the rind of some fruit.

Now he twists like a corkscrew
and falls, a headwater
for his own river of blood.

His assailant wiping his knife
with his sleeve, smiles,
and I sit straight up in bed.

The course of the sun through
the window runs right towards me.
Relief—my son and I are no where near

Bosnia, Herzegovina; yet
outside gulls wheel and scream
like Muslim women bereft of their sons.

Here we are caught lying in blood.
And what is our way out?
I watch a skein of geese

with their long, black necks
and side-slashed white beaks
wing their way over

the rough edges of the lake.
They land nearby, march in formation
across the beach assembling

for the long flight, instinctively
knowing how to winter away
from their own destruction.

Sandy in Washington D.C. with CODEPINK
and International Women for Peace marchers, March 2003

Dreams Blossom

March 2003
International Women's Day

*Don't be a victim, don't be a perpetrator, but beyond
all else, don't be a bystander.*
—a Jewish admonition

The cherry blossoms readying to bloom.
Thousands of women are back in D.C. marching

from Malcolm Park down Pennsylvania Avenue
to the fenced-off White House. Puffy clouds float over

us on this brilliant day and hundreds of honking cars,
our pink berets bobbing like white caps on waves

as we move along in support of peace.
The air of spring mingles with our wild hopes

of influencing at least our female representatives
to advocate against for war, to find a different solution.

Hilary Clinton meets our delegation. We plead, *Don't
send us to war in Iraq. It will be another Vietnam.*

She rebuffs us, boasting she has more information
than we do about weapons of mass destruction.

Days later, we know all our efforts are for naught.
On TV the hairs of Baghdad stand on end

before all is consumed by bombs dropped
into that ancient world, its history, its people—destroyed.

Every time another war starts, I feel
a whirring in the air, as if one could hear

the Earth turning on its axis collapsing.
My weight is thin parchment,

unable to ward off war. Before I die,
I want to see all empires renounce

violence, stop these endless, never ending wars.
What we need is a revolution of spirit.

How else will we all join as one
and the natural world remain a sanctuary

and the cherry blossoms finally
bloom in peace?

A Salute to Ruth Bader Ginsburg, Associate Justice of the United States Supreme Court

Ruth

Unknown to me, just a little older than I, you were my

Twin spirit. What a crazy idea we had as young women. The response?

Ha, ha, ha. You want to do what?

Become a lawyer. Women are not supposed to be lawyers,

After all, they must marry, carry babies,

Decide what to cook for dinner. (And ironing shirts takes much time too.)

End this fantasy, I was told, and you probably were told that too.

Risk so much if you go to law school. You will

Gather so much trouble around yourself, folks added.

It will be the path to the destruction of your femininity.

Not a single law firm will hire you, whether you're first in your class or not,

So listen. You didn't, I didn't either.

But that is another story for you, at least another chapter for me.

Ultimately, equality for women— more of it for us—one of your biggest
     accomplishments.

Rising to the highest court in the land. So respected, but for me
     I also understand so well the

Ground you first stood on. *Brava*, dear Ruth, *Brava*.

Looking Out Before the Next Election

2008
Minneapolis, Minnesota

I've come within a hairsbreadth
of history. What has it taught me?
A fistful of trees tense outside my window,
the elaborate feelings of space.
Inanimate objects glide inside the house.
This isn't the shallow bowl of my imagination.
No, everything is breaking.

I remember on a recent afternoon
Obama was on the stump without a tie.
McCain was riding in his bus and I
was preparing to be cloistered with nuns
who held themselves together
with straight pins and prayers. My hopes
were like something a scriptwriter would dream up.
I was destined to disappointment and
the corridors led to dead ends. Light falls

back from the window. A breeze lifts
the curtains. Born during the Christian calendar,
I've lived in a very secular age. The hippies
turned into Reaganites, then the Clintons paired up
with a triangle. Why be a barefoot
troublemaker any more? I won't make it
through the elaborate security checks.

It is so strange. Should I vote again?
Is there truth in the Bible, Koran,
Bhagavad Gita? What choice do I have,
but to stay here in my backyard,
drugged by the wildflowers,
the sanctity of it all?

Pandemic

The house is quiet. What might be
said is never ending

and my dog in his curl
by the fireplace is silent.

Wars will erupt
regardless,

and viruses will spread
on the world's breath.

You live in a parallel universe;
neither you nor your dog

will move mountains.
An algorithm from

some higher power
is urgently needed.

You might find salvation
if you wait until

the last leaf falls,
the dog speaks,

or the skies open,
filling you

with the vision
you seek.

This probably won't happen.
Patience.

A future is still possible.
Plan for it.

Space

April 2020

> *In my room, the world is beyond my understanding*
> —*"Of the Surface of Things,"* Wallace Stevens

During this lockdown I walk from room to room
in my condo, worried about whether I have
enough rooms. All this space now encompasses
seven continents. Along with Italy

and maybe Spain. The United States takes every inch
of my living and dining room. Canada must be on the porch.
England is surely in my bedroom and Boris Johnson,
recovering from the coronavirus, in the guest room.

I don't know where I'm going to put the 30,000-plus dead,
as my closets are filled with coats to stave off the winter chill.
And now there are more than half a million who
have been touched by this deadly virus, its little prickly
flower hovering right outside my door.

My anxiety rises as more people are getting
sick and dying, and now so many are losing their jobs.
My kitchen being of modest size, I certainly won't have enough
to feed them. I'm not even going to think about my bedrooms,
how many other desperate people could rest their heads here.

My car sits idle in my underground garage. I don't go out
for groceries, thanks to a son who delivers. But worst of all,
like some magnetic force, I'm drawn to turn on the TV,
only to see and hear from a man I would have quarantined
from any form of public office.

I haven't had wine or dined with family or friends,
seen a movie or laughed thinking my world is still fine.
Maybe I can clear all this up if I just turn off the TV.
Ah, now then, where is reality?

Work to Be Done

In memory of George Floyd

Tear gas defiles the air the sun departs

                             standoffish

marchers shouting

        of injustice

   shouting

        as darkness falls

plexiglass helmeted guardsmen race toward them

we cannot say   anything   they will hear

we cannot explain why justice has lost

        so much air

           has gone up

in smoke

               will-of-the wisp hopes

not heard

    beaten over the head

        the pounding feet

           of outrage

running every which way

        burning trash

    smothering smoke

shadowy figures dressed like spiders

skitter through webs of broken places

crawl over
    the wafting hopes of change we call for

on this dark night

    with no answers to be found
                    in these smoldering streets

Exposed in Minnesota

As a spring storm begins to rumble outside, I wrap
my dog in his thunder shirt, yet I must remain calm
and unprotected from what bears down
on us, whether it is thunder, city coyotes howling,
or the probable headlines of the *Star Tribune*—
the paper flung outside my door this morning,
as every day, by a man, whose young children wait
in his idling car. The fate of George Floyd's murderer
is soon to be determined by twelve citizens barricaded
in a courtroom behind barbed wire, as are the halls
of Congress, precautions against returning mobs, sicced
on the representatives of our frail democracy
by a crazed president who we supposedly ushered out
the door. But what to do about the cop who puts his knee—
for nine minutes—on the neck of a Black man,
smothering him, stopping all our lives, turning us
to marching in the streets, while troublemakers—homegrown,
or blown into Minneapolis—set the city streets and stores on fire,
inciting chaos among thousands of protesters, many of us
now realizing we need other gods or old gods to appear,
to stop us from killing each other, we who are filled with love,
hate, hope, and despair, stirred up by the Furies—
so little to protect us? All I can do is close the window
against the thunder, the smells of rain-dampened debris,
study the snow almost gone from the ground, now newly bare.

America, America

Winter winds, yes, they whistle, rattle
my windowpanes, blow cold
over our broken land,
but this country is bound
together, no matter the color
of our skins, our different histories.
We have sent out to the world our root music,
especially the strumming and the stomping
sown in our soil of strife.
Leadbelly, John Lee Hooker, stretch
the tensions out.
The rants of Jerry Lee Lewis,
the moves of Chubby Checkers,
the sweet refrains of Louie Armstrong sooth
our weary bones, while we swear
with Nina Simone—
this country keeps moving to the end
of the line with the Traveling Wilburys
or Bob Dylan on that train to New Orleans.
And let's not forget the electric
cords of Jim Morrison. America, America—
we are never bored with you.
You are *The Beautiful* even though *you ain't*
nothin' but a hound dog,
you are still mine. You are ours.
We are all bound to this land
and *that's alright. It's alright.*

Turbulence

Time sweeps everything away. Its lessons buried with lives lost. Rubble remains to stumble across, and stories survive only in shards. Sometimes a gale pounds into my sleep, and, by the force of its breath, denudes my dreams of speech, trees with only a tatter of leaves. Window ajar, I rise to listen. I must remember what can be remembered. Survival carries an obligation not to forget.

After Adam Zagajevski

A Better World

I trouble over the shadows
still hanging from trees—
American violence,
the darkness of our history,
even my own family's blindness—
so little understanding,
although long ago there were
Quaker ancestors in my family.
And how can I dismiss
what more I could have done
if I had been braver?

If only slavery hadn't become
so profitable, racism
would not have bloomed
like some invasive species,
seemingly impossible to beat
back or completely tear out.

Here on Earth, it's possible to turn away
from suffering, to think we can
create a world without it or ignore it,
but we can't have the stars
without the night.

I wonder, looking up into the dark
heavens, how I can be free
if you are not? Are the multitude
of stars sentinels for a better world?
A world so expansive that every soul—
not mine, not yours, but ours—
would be one united
universe of care?

2

Blanche has been gone for so long,
but even now I think of her,
how she might have fared
somewhat better in this century.

Some changes have come about,
and her great-granddaughter
might, at this moment, be looking out
her window and speaking
into the dark night and those stars—
as I did long ago—saying,

*Someday I'll go out and change
this world.* And maybe
she will.

AFTERWORD

This book is dedicated to Blanche Rice. She was a frequent presence at my grandparent's house. Hired as a domestic servant, she was treated nicely but was somehow separate from us because she was Black.

I loved her and felt that anyone who was older than your parents and seemed to love you as they did, would qualify as a grandmother. Privately, I thought of her as "my sideways grandmother," something I never said out loud. I may have thought that this was a "sideways" view, given the racial beliefs of most white adults in my world.

About four years ago, 2018, I read early versions of "In a more Privileged Place I" and "In a More Privileged Place II" to my Foreword Poetry group. These poems attempt to illustrate my befuddlement, starting at a young age, about what that separateness meant. As I became a teen, I began to see how this false idea of race created disparities of opportunity between whites and Blacks in New Jersey.

As I finished reading the second poem, I was asked by my fellow poets. "OK, this is interesting, so what happened next, what did you do about this?"

This book of poems came about because of that challenge.

A poet has two ways to approach writing a poem. The first and most inspiring is to sit down and begin writing when a line or an image pops into your head, then seeing where those images lead. The second is to start writing a poem with a topic already in mind, a challenge if the muse does not strike. Given that I was attempting to describe my struggle with racism as I grew up and my work on the issue as an adult, I began with the latter strategy. And I kept writing, tossing out and starting over, because how does one, in poetry, describe a sense of loss, a sense of outrage, a sense of expectation for better times when the muse is a bit elusive?

And as the personal is inextricably intertwined with the political and historical events of one's life experience, I began to incorporate these other public issues into my poetry as well. While wrestling with racism, inequity, and violence, we are also grappling with environmental degradation, sexism, homophobia, and now the world-wide pandemic. Another book would be needed if all these issues were to be explored in poetry. I hope the muse struck well enough to make the poems and pieces I have included here worthy of reflection.

As noted, most of these poems were written before 2020. The brutal murder of George Floyd on May 25, 2021, by the police in my home city of Minneapolis became a shape-shifting moment in history, as did the arrival of the deadly COVID-19 worldwide pandemic, the latter highlighting other issues of the day, and most recently the war in Ukraine.

I have held for a long time the painful view that the white world does not understand either our country's history or the destructive forces still weighing on people of color, most particularly African Americans. I welcome this sea change in attention to our racism and the inequity that it creates. I look forward with some optimism as my generation passes on the torch to younger generations. And I can only wish that, if or when a more just and peaceful era comes into view, the poetry of protest and celebration will continue to be crafted and will grapple with the challenges and threats unfolding on the horizon.

Sandra S. Larson

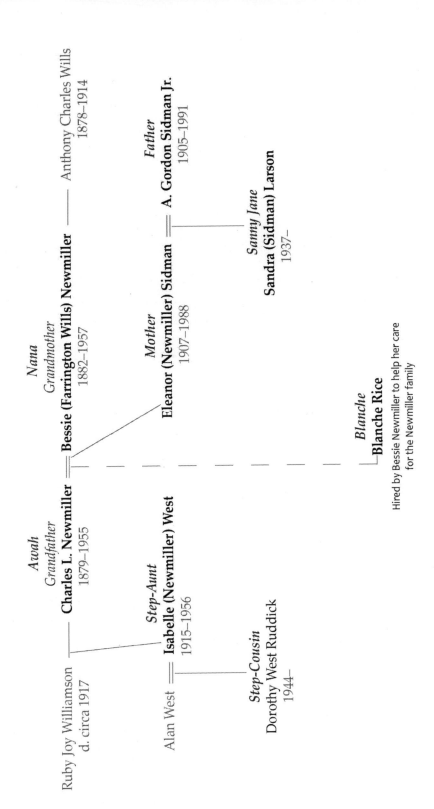

Awah
Grandfather
Charles L. Newmiller
1879–1955

Ruby Joy Williamson
d. circa 1917

Nana
Grandmother
Bessie (Farrington Wills) Newmiller
1882–1957

Anthony Charles Wills
1878–1914

Step-Aunt
Isabelle (Newmiller) West
1915–1956

Alan West

Step-Cousin
Dorothy West Ruddick
1944–

Mother
Eleanor (Newmiller) Sidman
1907–1988

Father
A. Gordon Sidman Jr.
1905–1991

Sanny Jane
Sandra (Sidman) Larson
1937–

Blanche
Blanche Rice
Hired by Bessie Newmiller to help her care
for the Newmiller family

This is a chart of the family member relationships mentioned in this book.
If it were a family tree, additional family members would appear including
Sandra's sibling, Shirley (Sidman) Hogan and Dorothy's siblings, Alan West Jr. and Diane (West) Morino.

NOTES

"Awakening"

This poem was written in April 2022, as the seeming obliteration of Ukraine by Russian forces was underway, and after reading Naomi Shihab Nye's poem "Kindness" (from *The Words Under the Words: Selected Poems*. Eighth Mountain Press, 1995).

"What Remains"

The devastation of the September 21, 1938 hurricane went beyond Misquamicut, Rhode Island. However, all 400 homes in Misquamicut were washed away, and 41 people died. It is estimated that between 600–800 people throughout New England and Long Island lost their lives. A total of 8,000 homes were destroyed and 6,000 boats. The storm did damage from Long Island to Maine, submerging Providence, Rhode Island, in its wake.

While this storm brewing off the coast of Africa had been spotted by storm-trackers, radar had not been invented in 1938. Unfortunately, the trackers erred in their judgment as to the path it would take. They predicted it would not make landfall along the coast of New England. It was a beautiful September day—until it wasn't.

Most of the lives that were lost came from the tidal wave that accompanied the storm. The disaster has been largely forgotten, perhaps, because there was no time to linger on it after the events that led to WWII arrived one month later. Sudetenland, a large section of Czechoslovakia, was annexed by Hitler's Germany in October 1938; the invasion of Poland by Hitler came only one year later in the fall of 1939.

It wasn't until the early 1950s that the U.S. National Hurricane Center first developed a formal practice for storm naming for the Atlantic Ocean. The stories of this disaster, called The Great New England Hurricane of 1938 after it occurred, was the worst in New England history. The *1938 Hurricane Along New England's Coast* by Joseph P. Soares, documents the destruction caused by the 1938 hurricane along New England's coast and the ways in which victims united to rebuild their communities. (Arcadia Publishing, 2008).

"The Distance of Trouble"

"Screaming Mimis" were German rocket guns, "Nebelwerfers," mounted on a half-track that fired in clusters of six or twelve, a second and a half apart.

The noise of the incoming rockets led the Allied forces to give them nicknames. I mistakenly called them "meanies."

Mussolini and his mistress Claretta Petacci were executed on April 28, 1945, in Mezzegra, Italy, and their bodies hung upside down in a Milan plaza. Hitler committed suicide on April 30, 1945, in his underground bunker in Berlin. The bunker still exists in the middle of the city. It is unmarked so as not to be a tourist attraction. I have walked past it.

The first major concentration camp was discovered by the Soviets in 1944 in Poland. The remaining 7,000 prisoners were liberated from Auschwitz by the Soviet army on January 27, 1945. US forces liberated over 20,000 prisoners at Buchenwald in Germany on April 11, 1945. British forces liberated camps in northern Germany.

The US dropped two nuclear bombs over the Japanese cities of Hiroshima and Nagasaki on August 6 and August 9, 1945. Up to 236,000 citizens died. Japan surrendered to the Allies on August 15, 1945, thus ending WWII.

"Skating Away"

Hans Brinker or The Silver Skates (full title: *Hans Brinker; or, the Silver Skates: A Story of Life in Holland*) is a novel by American author Mary Mapes Dodge. First published in 1865, it has been in continuous publication since then. The novel is set in mid-19th century Netherlands and contains not only the story of Hans and his skates but another story—more famous than the tales about Hans. It is the the story of the little Dutch boy who plugged a dike and saved his country from flooding.

"In a More Privileged Place II"

Memory is tricky. As a teen I thought the *Life* magazine photo essay on a Harlem family was done by Gordon Parks in the 1950s, but now I realize he did that shoot in 1968. By then, I was married and had three children. I did see an article about a poor African American family, if not in *Life*, then in some other magazine during my teen years.

Some of my father's Dutch ancestors came to New Amsterdam shortly after it was settled in 1624; therefore I assume some of them might have lived in the area now known as Harlem.

"A Wider World Comes Into View"

There are enumerable media reports and historical references to this crime on Wikipedia and other Google sites. Homer's tales of the Cyclops can be found in his epic poem the *Odyssey*, believed to have been written in the 8th century BCE.

"What Was Unearthed Today"

Not only did Cronkite dominate the TV news of this "Freedom Riders" tragedy, but he was the narrator of the JFK assassination and its dramatic aftermath.

Andrew Goodman and Michael Schwerner were both white, while James Chaney was African American. The murderers were largely known. Subsequently seven were found guilty of federal civil rights violations. Only six went to prison; none served more than six years. Finally, Killen, the mastermind of the plot who had walked free, was brought to trial again, found guilty of three counts of manslaughter, and sentenced to 60 years in prison. He died there. The Hollywood movie *Mississippi Burning* tells the story of the search for justice for the three murdered men and their families. The PBS *American Experience* documentary "Freedom Riders" covers this tragedy.

An underreported side story of this event was that more Black bodies were uncovered when the authorities went digging for the three civil rights workers: two college students identified as Moore and Dee, a 14-year-old identified as Herbert Oarsby, and five Mississippi men never identified. Their murders were not investigated.

"The Insufferable Summer of Urban Riots with the War Dead Continuing to Return Home"

While the early 1960s saw numerous urban riots, starting in June 1967, 159 "race riots" erupted that year alone in cities throughout the United States. In Newark 26 people were killed during these riots over four days of the conflict from July 12 through July 17. The National Guard was called out to occupy the city with tanks and other military equipment.

The year 1967 was not the end of the unrest. In 1968, six more American cities erupted into destructive riots sparked largely that year by the assassinations of Martin Luther King and Robert Kennedy.

"Roots: Found Poem Written After Reading the Narrative of a Former Slave's Experience"

The collection *Born in Slavery: Slave Narratives from the Federal Writers' Project, 1936-1938* contains more than 2,300 first-person accounts of slavery and 500 black-and-white photographs of former slaves. These narratives were collected in the 1930s as part of the Federal Writers' Project (FWP) of the Works Progress Administration later renamed Work Projects Administration (WPA).

"Upon the Occasion of the United States Congress Passing a Resolution in 2005 Apologizing for Having Done Nothing to Prevent the 4,742 Lynchings After the Civil War"

On June 13, 2005, the US Senate finally passed a resolution of apology to the nearly 5,000 people and their descendants documented as lynched since 1880. This resolution also apologized for never having made lynching a federal crime. Over 200 such bills were presented to the US House of Representatives between 1890 and 1952; three were passed out of the House to the Senate, where they all met with defeat. *ABC News*, June 13, 2005.

See S.Res.39, 109th Congress. Also see text of S.J.Res. 14, 111th Congress, which served as the basis for Layli Long Soldier's book *Whereas*.

There are other articles on the Internet about this struggle.

"In a Carceral State"

John Ehrlichman, Richard Nixon's domestic policy chief, was quoted as saying in a1994 interview he had with Dan Baum in *Harper's* magazine, "We knew we couldn't make it illegal to be either against the war or blacks, but by getting the public to associate the hippies with marijuana and blacks with heroin, and then criminalizing both heavily, we could disrupt those communities … Did we know we were lying about drugs? Of course, we did."

Some dispute he meant this, but this strategy seemed to be one of the triggers for a much greater emphasis on incarceration throughout the United States that inordinately effected African American men. There is also a complex tie with the enslaved labor of the plantations that changed after the Civil War only in that Black men and women were then no longer technically slaves, but they worked as abused tenant farmers and farm hands well after emancipation.

Natchez, Mississippi, was a hub of not only the growth of cotton but a shipping center as it was located on the lower Mississippi River. It was the wealthiest city in the United States during this period, and many mansions and large churches were built with the expectation it would remain so. It was very much interlinked with the industrial north that relied on the cotton for its factories.

Many Northerners also owned plantations and thus had a direct interest in the perpetration of slavery.

"A Visit to 15 Parkway, Upper Montclair, New Jersey"

My step-grandfather was of German descent which makes me think that "Awah" was a mispronunciation of "Opa," the German word for "grandfather."

"Four Children in the Picture"

Jacob Lawrence, an African American artist, painted a series of pictures based on the great migration of Africans in the first decades of the twentieth century from the south to the north in search of better lives. This great upheaval in American society is well chronicled in Pulitzer Prize winning Isabel Wilkerson's book *The Warmth of Other Suns*.

"Dinner at the Edge of the Empire"

The Green Berets were a Special Forces arm of the US Army organized in 1952 to undertake unconventional warfare. Their nickname was given them by John F. Kennedy, when he ordered the green beret be used as their field headgear. They were the first deployed secretly to Vietnam in 1961 to help the South Vietnamese Army fight the insurgent North Vietnamese-organized Viet Cong. The South Vietnamese Army was officially named the Army of the Republic of Vietnam (ARVN). In the 14 years from the entrance of the Green Berets into the combat zone until the fall of Saigon in 1975, 58,000 Americans lost their lives while 1.1 million North Vietnamese soldiers and civilians and 2.25 million South Vietnamese soldiers and citizens lost theirs.

"If the Impossible Is Possible"

President John F. Kennedy was assassinated on November 22, 1963, while riding in a motorcade in Dallas with his wife and the governor of Texas John Connelly. Jackie's famously blood-stained pink suit is now stored in an unknown location. Her hat was never found.

Many conspiracy theories abound as to whether the lethal gunshots came only from Oswald in the Texas Book Depository or whether there were other snipers either there or elsewhere at the scene. The motivations for this murder are still unclear.

Also, some historians have postulated from various statements that President Kennedy made that he would not have sent regular ground troops into Vietnam. If that were so, we would not have fought and lost that diabolical war.

"Seasons of Memory"

Washington, D.C. citizens and public figures were attempting to plant trees along the mall at the turn of the twentieth century. To aid in this effort over 2,000 cherry trees were donated by Mayor Yukio Ozaki from the City of Tokyo as a goodwill gesture in March of 1912. The story is available through Wikipedia and other Google sites.

The Bataan Death March was a horrendous forced march of about 60 miles by the Japanese of American and Filipino war prisoners from one prison camp in the Philippine Islands to another. It began on April 9, 1942. The distance was about sixty miles, but the physical abuse, starvation, and killing inflicted by the Japanese along the way was enough to have the treatment of these prisoner adjudicated as a war crime. My mother's cousin died from the lingering effects of having been a prisoner on this march.

"Imploding on the News While Reading T. S. Eliot's "The Wasteland""

In response to Iraq's invasion and annexation of Kuwait in August 1990, President George H. W. Bush assembled a coalition of 35 nations to launch a war to restore Kuwait's sovereignty. He was widely quoted justifying the war saying it was motivated *by a big idea—a new world order*. He described it as being solidly against aggression, for peaceful settlement of disputes … and for the just treatment of all people. To many of us, it appeared more like a war fueled by the idea of American exceptionalism and the administration's keen desire to control the production and distribution of Middle Eastern oil.

When I was watching this horrific war devolve into chaos, Eliot's "Wasteland" and its poetic imagery seemed apt. The war was largely directed and funded by the US, but coalition countries did provide equipment and personnel. The French supplied their aging jet fighter planes the Dassault Mirage 2000. The desert locale also tied the war and poem together. As is well know, there was a second Gulf War, during President George W. Bush's term. The US invaded Iraq in 2003 due to unfounded suspicions that Iraqi ruler Saddam Hussein had weapons of mass destruction. While this poem was largely written in response to viewing the horrors of the first Gulf War on TV, I expanded the poem later on and added the imagery of Baghdad being blown up on March 13, 2003. The spiking flare reminded me of Eliot's lines … *her hair | spread out in fiery points.*

"Morning Witness"

The "Kosovo War" was fought between the Federal Republic of Serbia (Serbia and Montenegro) and the Kosovo Albanian rebel group known as the Kosovo Liberation Army (KLA). It began in late February 1998, and ended June 11, 1999, with the acceptance of the Kumanovo Agreement. The warring factions prompted an intervention of NATO that was controversial in many quarters. Over 13,500 people were killed or went missing during the two-year conflict.

It was the reportage on this carnage that prompted my nightmare, which triggered this poem.

"Dreams Blossom"

A war in Iraq appeared more imminent after the US Congress passed a resolution in October 2002, authorizing President George W. Bush to launch a military attack against Iraq, if he decided it was necessary. The International Association of Women based in Geneva, Switzerland, with chapters throughout the US, and CODEPINK, a grassroots women's organization working to end US wars and militarism, joined forces in 2003. Their aim: organize a protest in Washington, DC, and visit with congressional representatives, particularly women representatives, to plead woman to woman, not to invade Iraq.

The leading figure in this protest coalition was Medea Benjamin, an American political activist and Green Party US Senate candidate in 2000 from California. She dubbed her women for peace group CODEPINK making its name a play on the US Department of Homeland Security color-coded system (orange, red, etc.), which was designed to alert the public to terrorist threats after 9/11. "Code Pink" was also the color code hospitals used when staff thought a child might have been abducted from the hospital.

Two prominent writers at this event were Alice Walker and Maxine Hong Kingston. I was honored to march with these dedicated women.

"Looking Out Before the Next Election"

Candidates in the 2008 presidential election were Barack Obama, Democrat, and John McCain, Republican. I was nervous about the outcome when I wrote this poem, and although the results were what I wanted, the eight years ahead were both challenging and disappointing.

"A Salute to Ruth Bader Ginsburg, Associate Justice of the United States Supreme Court"

This poem was written only months before Justice Ginsburg's death on September 18, 2020, at eighty-six. She was very well-known for her legal successes expanding equal rights for women during her illustrious legal career prior to joining the high court. She was the second woman to sit on the Supreme Court, serving from 1993 until her death. Movies, documentaries, and other sources chronicle her exceptional life.

"Pandemic" and "Space"

These two poems were both written rather early-on during the global coronavirus pandemic that caused lockdown throughout the United States beginning in March 2020. It was, perhaps, a period more of confusion than despair for those of us lucky enough to have the resources and the ability to shelter in place.

"Work to be Done"

When the disruptions broke out in Minneapolis after the infamous video of George Floyd's death at the hands of Minneapolis police, given the pandemic and also my age, I joined the protest in spirit and stayed glued to the TV all night. It brought back memories of the frightening moments of the Vietnam protests in Washington, D.C., I did attend, so many years back. I despaired at the destruction that went on, but even more, I saw again how police have little training in deescalating a situation. Instead, their aggressive and often brutal acts inflame and wound protesters, and they, in turn, can be injured.

"Exposed in America'

This was written on the night when the crowds were out on the streets of Minneapolis awaiting the judicial decisions about the fate of Derek Chauvin who was found guilty of murdering George Floyd in April 20, 2021. The outcome brought a sense of relief to this beleaguered city.

"America, America"

All those named are singers, songwriters and musicians born and most widely known in the 20th century. Some are still alive and thriving in 2022, such as Bob Dylan. Huddie William Ledbetter, better known as "Lead Belly," was born in 1880 and was one of the fathers of the blues. Louis Armstrong, who was born in 1901 and died in 1971, was also one of the most influential African American musicians of his time.

Many American songsters have used the phrase "it's all right" in their lyrics or titles such as Bob Dylan's song "Don't Think Twice, It's All Right." However, the original American song with this title was written by African American musician Curtis Mayfield. "It's Alright" was first recorded by The Impressions in 1963. I also sing along with the Traveling Wilburys' (of which Dylan was a member) popular hit "End of the Line," with its repeating phrase, "Well, it's alright, ridin' around in the breeze."

"Turbulence"

This poem was prompted, in part, by lines from Adam Zagajewski's poem "Shells" that Clare Cavanagh translated into English (from *Mysticism for Beginners: Poems* (Macmillan, Apr 15, 1999):

> ... Time takes life away
> and gives us memory, gold with flame,
> black with embers.

ACKNOWLEDGMENTS

I am delighted that Leslie Matton-Fynn is my editor and publisher of this, my third full-length volume. I am indebted to her for shepherding my efforts with this book, from layout design, to editing, researching and fact checking, to publishing, all under the banner of her company, Cup and Spiral Books, Minneapolis, Minnesota. We met through our involvement with the Loft Literary Center here in Minneapolis many years ago and have remained together in our ongoing poetry circle, The Foreword Poetry Group. As a poet herself, Leslie's suggestions have strengthened my poems and her design skills makes this book, with its print design and pictures, a visual work of art. With such a deep feeling of gratitude, I thank you, Leslie.

Many workshop poetry teachers along the way, especially at the Loft Literary Center of Minneapolis, have helped me improve my craft. My first teacher and ongoing mentor for many years, Roseann Lloyd, has also been a gracious reader of this new collection. With this volume I have drawn in one of my early and very influential poetry teachers, Margaret Hasse, whose poetry I have admired over the years. I was delighted when she agreed to review this volume for me. Not only did she read the manuscript so as to write a review, she also gave it a very close reading and offered many helpful suggestions to strengthen it. Thank you, Margaret.

Two accomplished and acclaimed poets, Jude Nutter and Thomas R. Smith have mentored our Foreword Poetry Group—one or the other of them—once a month over the last eleven years. I wouldn't be where I am today without the help I received from Jude Nutter as I began to think about publishing a full-length manuscript. Without Jude's guidance *This Distance in My Hands* would not have seen the light of day.

And for this book, Thomas R. Smith has been such a source of inspiration and encouragement. He has thoughtfully and thoroughly gone through the first version of this manuscript, the second, and the third! I doubt this book would have been created without his insightful suggestions and encouragement. Many thanks to Thomas for your editing and confirming this collection had something to say about the joys and sorrows of living through these times.

As noted, our Foreword Poetry Group has met twice monthly for eleven years, more recently via Zoom. I am so fond of and indebted to: Stephanie Brown, Sue Crouse, Barbara Draper, Kristin Laurel, Leslie Matton-Flynn, Ardie Medina,

LeRoy Sorenson, William Upjohn, and Miriam Weinstein. I must single out Stephanie for being willing to evaluate and advise me on this current volume as she did my last. Her insights are always significant ones. So thankful for your help, Steph.

I have friends not in my poetry circles who have read and reacted to various drafts of this book. They are Lee Henry Jordan, Karen Wadman, and Dolores Schaefer. Karen and Dolores both volunteered to copy edit my manuscript. Both Karen and Dolores are retired college professors, Karen an English professor and Dolores, a French professor. As the major organizer for our Minneapolis Juneteenth celebration and a poet in his own right, I was also very happy to have Lee's prospective and advice. Thank you Dee, Karen, and Lee.

I have had the good fortune this past year of working with a reconstituted group of poets that we used to call The Painted Chair Poets. Thank you, Mary Junge, Shannon King, Carol Rucks, and June Blumenson for your insights regarding numerous poems in this collection.

I also want to give thanks and credit to two fellow poets that are no longer with us. Thomas Heie, the beloved editor and owner of a small local press, Sidewalks, passed away in January of 2021. Tom was one of the first editors to accept my poems as I first began to send them out. The second poet friend and colleague I miss is James Bettendorf. Jim was one of my Foreword Poetry Group members who died in February of 2021. We worked together for eleven years. His absence is still a big hole in our poetry circle and in my heart.

PUBLICATION ACKNOWLEDGMENTS

The following poems, some in slightly different form, have appeared in earlier publications and online:

"A Child's Welfare," "[Dad] Who's To Know What Will Happen Next"; *This Distance In My Hands*, Main Street Rag Publishing Company, Charlotte, NC 2017

"Exposed," *The New Verse. News*, Monday, March 29, 2021

"Four Children In The Picture"; *In the Company of Others*, Cup and Spiral Books, Minneapolis, MN 2017

"Looking Out Before The Next Election", *The International Times* posted on 7 May, 2015, https://internationaltimes.it/looking-out-before-the-next-election/

"In A More Privileged Place I" (as "Etiquette at Nana's House"), "[Dad] Now What Will We Do?", "Seasons of Memory", "Whistling Girls And Cackling Hens Always Come To Some Bad End"; *Whistling Girls and Cackling Hens*, Pudding House Publications, Columbus, OH, 2003

"Pandemic", *The New Verse. News* posted on 27 March, 2020, https://newversenews.blogspot.com/2020/03/pandemic.html

"Space," *A 21st Century Plague: Poetry from a Pandemic*, edited by Elayne Cliff, University Professors Press, Colorado Springs, CO, 2021

"The Distance of Trouble", "What Usually Is Seen as too Small to Mention"; *Over the Threshold of Roots*, Pudding House Publications, Columbus, OH, 2007

And Now What Shall We Do?

ISBN 979-8-9868154-0-4

Printed in the United States of America
Copyright © 2022 by Sandra Sidman Larson

For permission and information contact
Sandra Sidman Larson at slpoet47@gmail.com

Book design and layout, editor: Leslie Matton-Flynn
Cup and Spiral Books, Minneapolis, MN

All photographs property of Sandra Sidman Larson

CUP & SPIRAL BOOKS
MINNEAPOLIS ✿ MINNESOTA